Original title:
Wormhole Whimsy

Copyright © 2025 Creative Arts Management OÜ
All rights reserved.

Author: Christian Leclair
ISBN HARDBACK: 978-1-80567-797-0
ISBN PAPERBACK: 978-1-80567-918-9

The Lore of Luminous Larks

In a sky made of giggles, larks take flight,
With feathers of sparkle, they dance in the night.
They swoop through the stars, in a whimsical swirl,
Chasing their tails, in a cosmic twirl.

They sing to the moon, with a voice like a joke,
Each note a confetti, each chuckle a poke.
Their laughter erupts like a fizzy drink,
As they bounce on the clouds, and make stars wink.

Bouncing through realms where the strange is the norm,
They juggle comets while dodging a storm.
With giggles that echo in galaxies wide,
They play hide and seek with a bright shooting star's ride.

With every new leap, they plow through the air,
A ruckus of joy, without any care.
In a universe silly, where fun never ends,
These larks teach us laughter is what life intends.

Starlight Shenanigans

In the night sky, twinkling bright,
Stars play tag, a silly sight.
Comets dash with goofy glee,
Dance in circles, wild and free.

Planets wobble, laugh and spin,
Jumping jacks beneath their skin.
Galaxies swirl in dizzy cheer,
Whispers of fun, loud and clear.

Temporal Teeter-totters

On a seesaw of time, we go,
Up and down, oh what a show!
Yesterday's jokes tickle today,
While tomorrow just wants to play.

Clock hands spinning like a top,
Giggles echo, never stop.
Future slips on bananas peels,
Time to laugh at how it feels.

Frivolous Forays into the Unknown

Let's jump through doors that twist and twirl,
Chasing laughter, giving it a whirl.
Dimensions with cotton candy skies,
Where silly creatures wear disguise.

Upside-down and sideways too,
In this realm, we twist and skew.
Maps made of jelly, paths of cream,
Step right in, it's all a dream!

The Funhouse of Forever

In a house of mirrors, jokes reflect,
Laughter bounces, what's to expect?
Wobbling walls that giggle and shake,
Every turn a new mistake.

Eternity's tickles, a playful tease,
With puzzling paths that aim to please.
Hopscotch across the endless floor,
Foolish fun forevermore!

The Joy of Interstellar Wandering

In a rocket made of jellybeans,
I zoom past stars and dancing moons.
The aliens wave with fluffy hands,
While we share tunes from strange lands.

I traded my shoes for a comet's tail,
And laughed as I rode a cosmic whale.
Eating stardust popcorn, I grin wide,
No traffic, just joy on this galactic ride.

Whimsical Worlds Unseen

Beneath the rings of a candy realm,
I found a frog who loves to helm.
He croaked a tune of gummy dreams,
Souring the silence with beetle beams.

In fields of marshmallow grass we played,
Chasing sparkly critters that never stayed.
With lollipop trees and syrupy streams,
This universe sprinkles wild, sweet themes.

The Zany Ziggurat of Space

Up on a tower made of macarons,
I juggled planets until they yawned.
The nebulae giggled, swirling with glee,
As I danced like a freaky space flea.

With every leap, I'd bounce and glide,
On jellyfish clouds, I took a wild ride.
Wobbling by stars that shimmer and shine,
In the ziggurat's laugh, I felt divine.

Adventures in Celestial Chronicles

There once was a knight with a popcorn sword,
Fighting marshmallow foes with a cheerful chord.
Galactic quests on spaghetti trails,
Sailing through history with gummy whales.

Each chapter unfolds like a magic trick,
With silly sidekicks who prance and flick.
Through laughter and joy, I journey bright,
In chronicles where space feels just right.

Contra-Cosmic Capers

In a sock drawer, a portal hides,
Where cat toys dance on colorful rides.
Uncle Zog wears a hat made of cheese,
And juggles space lemons with perfect ease.

Galactic ducks waddle, quack in tune,
While a cow jumps over a neon moon.
They sip from cups of fizzy star juice,
And debate the best way to lose a moose.

A marble rolls down a cosmic slide,
With rubber band rockets, they all glide.
The rules of gravity take a vacation,
In this wacky, wild, star-studded nation.

So join the fun, don't be a bore,
There's laughter and chaos forevermore.
In this realm where silliness reigns,
Flip through galaxies, let go of your chains.

Lullabies from the Loop.

Tiny frogs on roller skates,
Sing soft songs to curious mates.
They twirl around in sleepy streams,
While lullabies weave through their dreams.

Mice in pajamas sip cocoa warm,
As chocolate rivers flow in the swarm.
A teddy bear flies on a kite,
Chasing moonbeams in the night.

Stars wink down with mischievous glee,
While clouds make friends and float like three.
A giggle erupts from a cosmic cat,
As time bends softly, imagine that!

In these loops where giggles abound,
Silly shadows dance all around.
Sleep comes gently, with a twist of fate,
In a world where night-time is never late.

Galactic Jester

A clown with eight arms spins around,
Launching confetti from barriers unbound.
He juggles planets, both big and small,
While a disco ball reflects it all.

Starships honk like geese in flight,
As they zip through dimensions, what a sight!
Each wacky turn brings silly delight,
In a carnival lost in the night.

Jumping beans in zero-G bounce,
While giggling aliens all announce:
The best joke yet beyond the sun,
"For a punchline, just squirt some fun!"

So let's all laugh and tip our hats,
To the galaxy's quirkiest acrobats.
In the cosmic circus, join the show,
Where humor's the currency, let it flow!

Time's Turbulent Tides

Tick-tock fish swim against the stream,
Dancing in loops, oh what a dream!
They wear hats made of clocks and cream,
And sip on tea with a wink and gleam.

Pages of time flip with a whoosh,
As dinosaurs skateboard in a big, wild swoosh.
With laughter, they race through time's great maze,
Leaving trails of giggles in a happy blaze.

Balloons fly past in colors bright,
While strange machines whirr in delight.
Nonsense rules in this playful spree,
As we twirl and spin, oh can't you see?

So come ride the waves of this whimsical tide,
Where time is a playground, come and slide.
In moments of chaos, we find our glee,
As laughter surrounds us, eternally free!

Cosmic Carousel

Galaxies spin on a merry-go-round,
Stars wear hats and dance all around.
Comets slide, playing peek-a-boo,
While black holes giggle, 'Who are you?'

Planets join in a cosmic parade,
Jupiter winks, donning a cascade.
Neptune flips pancakes, quite a delight,
As Mars juggles moons in the night.

Quantum Quirks

Electrons tap-dance, light feet aflame,
While photons whisper, 'We're not the same!'
Particles twirl in a playful race,
Entangled laughter fills the space.

Superposition in a silly hat,
Quantum cats purring, imagine that!
Mystery giggles in the fabric of time,
As theories twist in a whimsical rhyme.

Stellar Serenade

Shooting stars serenade the night,
Singing tunes that shimmer and bite.
Venus croons with a velvet voice,
While Saturn strums, giving us choice.

With cosmic beats from a neutron star,
Each melody echoes, near and far.
Celestial choirs in harmonized glee,
Invite us to dance in zero gravity.

Curled in the Cosmos

A nebula snuggles in a cloud of fluff,
While cosmic kittens know they are tough.
Starry-eyed dreams, all tangled in light,
Giggles cascade through the endless night.

Asteroids roll like bells on a spree,
Sprinkling stardust on all that we see.
Curled in the cosmos, we laugh and we play,
As time does a twirl, just whisking away.

Hyperspace Hijinks

In a rocket made of cheese,
The crew danced on their knees.
With laughter echoing wide,
They zoomed through the starry tide.

Asteroids wore silly hats,
As comets chased after cats.
Nebulae giggled in delight,
Turning the gloom into light.

A space whale sang a tune,
While stars juggled with the moon.
They raced against a solar flare,
And left behind a trail of flair.

The universe spins in a whirl,
As planets give a happy twirl.
In this fun and zany chase,
Every corner hides a new face.

A Voyage through Fantasia

On a ship of paper planes,
We sailed through colorful lanes.
With unicorns as our crew,
We painted the skies in blue.

Each cloud a candy burst,
In this realm of dreamers first.
Rainbows sprouted like balloons,
Tickling the sleepy moons.

A dragon offered us some cake,
While fairies danced by the lake.
The stars would flicker and cheer,
As we found joy over here.

Every turn brought a surprise,
With silly sights to mesmerize.
In this land of make-believe,
Laughter flows and we believe.

The Celestial Lark

A space bird with a trumpet call,
Sings goofy tunes to one and all.
With twinkling stars as backdrop bright,
It dances through the galaxy night.

Echoes of laughter ring so true,
As asteroids join in the view.
They tango with a wishing star,
In a whimsical jam afar.

Cosmic giggles fill the air,
While planets hop without a care.
Black holes wearing silly socks,
Swirl around with ticklish knocks.

In this grand celestial show,
Where winks and wobbles freely flow,
Every tune is an adventure bold,
In the cradle of galaxies untold.

Adventures in the Space Between

Bouncing through the cosmic gaps,
Fluffy clouds in funny wraps.
With aliens sporting oversized shoes,
They invite us to join their blues.

Time giggles as it flies,
While we dance beneath bright skies.
Gravity takes a playful leap,
As whimsical secrets we keep.

The void is filled with candy stars,
As spaceships rev their fuzzy cars.
Astro-jellybeans float around,
In this zany space we've found.

With trails of laughter in our wake,
We bake sunshine in a cake.
Adventures swirl into the night,
As joy travels with delight.

Twists of Cosmic Delight

In a swirl of fizzy light,
Cats in space put up a fight.
Chasing stars like shiny toys,
Giggles echo, cosmic noise.

Planets wobble, moons will twirl,
As space-time bends in a whirl.
Gravity plays tricks so sly,
Watch the comets zoom and fly.

With each twist, reality bends,
Laughter bursts, it never ends.
Aliens in hats parade,
In this dance, we're all dismayed.

So let's sip on starlight tea,
And toast to oddity with glee!
For in this cosmos, wild and bright,
We'll spin and twirl in sheer delight.

Paradoxical Playgrounds

Bouncing on a nebula swing,
Playing tag with a space-time king.
Flipping through dimensions bold,
In this playground, joy unfolds.

Slides made of stardust glow,
Each ride makes our giggles grow.
Asteroids are our bowling balls,
When cosmic antics fill the halls.

Jumping jacks with aliens green,
In this realm, we jest and preen.
A tickle from a comet's tail,
Sends us into an orbiting wail.

At dusk, the cosmos paints a smile,
With giggling stars, we'll stay awhile.
In this whimsical, absurd place,
Laughter echoes through endless space.

Interstellar Mischief

A cheeky star wore underpants,
As planets burst into silly dances.
With asteroids playing pranks,
Gravity travails in wild ranks.

Sprinkling moonbeams in our hair,
Dancing cows float with flair.
Giggles ripple through the air,
As noted ships go 'neigh!' without care.

Time-travel jokes and cosmic laughs,
Worms in spacesuits, making gaffes.
In orbits, chaos reigns supreme,
As we tangle in a wobbly dream.

So let's scribble doodles in the sky,
With comet trails that wink and sigh.
For mischief thrives in the endless blue,
And laughter's the secret, just between us two.

Dance of the Dimensional Dancer

Twisting through the fabric fine,
Dancer spreads her sparkly shine.
With each leap, the laws unbend,
As giggles greet each cosmic friend.

Stars to cha-cha, planets to boogie,
In this tune, no one's a rookie.
Galaxies whirl in a jolly spree,
With laughter echoing frivolously.

She spins on glimmers of delight,
Crafting joy from endless night.
Hopping through the dimensional seams,
Chasing after outlandish dreams.

So twirl with all your might and glee,
Join the fun, come dance with me!
In a lively shift, let spirits prance,
In this cosmic, whimsical dance.

The Spectrum of Spacetime

In a twisty turn of fate,
Time plays hide and seek with late.
A clock unwinds, a tick goes bloop,
As moments dance in a cosmic loop.

Jellybeans in starry skies,
Launch their rockets with silly cries.
A rainbow streaks across the dark,
Spaceship pilots trace a spark.

Gravity's got a playful hand,
Pulling comets like a band.
An asteroid with a goofy grin,
Dances with planets, spin and spin.

Warped realities bring a cheer,
With quirky friends, they gather near.
They laugh at time, what a delight,
In the spectrum of the cosmic night.

Fables from the Fifth Dimension

In spaces where the stories play,
Cats wear hats and dogs ballet.
Tales of worlds that twist and twine,
Fables woven into line.

A jellyfish sings a lullaby,
To stars that twinkle in the sky.
With zebra-striped spaceships, they glide,
Through dimensions, so much to bide.

A three-eyed frog with superpowers,
Counts the minutes, waits for hours.
He hops on clouds and makes a splash,
In a universe where dreams are brash.

Laughter echoes through the void,
As cosmic pets seek to avoid,
The mundane clock that ticks away,
In fables strange, they laugh and play.

Astral Escapades

Comets chase a shooting star,
While squids play piano from afar.
Bubbles rise in cosmic tea,
As aliens dance with glee.

A penguin waltzes on the Moon,
Painting craters, afternoon.
Galaxies with giggles show,
That even spacetime bends with flow.

Hot air balloons made of cheese,
Float through voids with utmost ease.
Laughing moons, they tip their hats,
To space-traveling, curious cats.

Explorers wear their socks on head,
While dreamers frolic in their bed.
In fun and whimsy, they unite,
In astral realms, they take their flight.

Echoing Laughter through the Stars

With echoes ringing through the space,
Giggles bounce from place to place.
A star's bright grin, a comet's wink,
In the void where all thoughts link.

A parade of planets spins around,
In joyful races, they're unbound.
Galactic jesters juggle light,
While stardust sprinkles through the night.

Tales are told by twinkling eyes,
Of mischievous suns and silly sighs.
Each laugh that travels far and wide,
Brings joy to those born to glide.

So come along, let's take a ride,
Through cosmic waves, we'll glide and slide.
In laughter shared, we'll journey fast,
Through echoing dreams, forever cast.

Spirited Spectacles

In the land where quarks all twirl,
And atoms wear a wiggly swirl,
A sock with stripes begins to sing,
As jellybeans sprout tiny wings.

A squirrel in shades on a pogo stick,
Jumps through time, it's quite the trick!
He winks and shrugs as he zips by,
While giggling stars light up the sky.

A teapot drips out rainbow tea,
That spills to form a lively sea,
Fish with feet dance on the shore,
While marshmallow clouds begin to snore.

So grab your hat, your funky shoes,
Join the party, heed the news!
In this realm, we're free to dance,
Life's a swirl of goofy chance!

The Hypnotic Dance of Dimensions

With a twist of light and a swirl of shade,
Time takes a break to join the parade,
Dancing sandwiches tap their feet,
As talking clocks groove to the beat.

A galaxy of giggles spins around,
In this wacky, whirling, cosmic ground,
Where pebbles juggle and planets prance,
And sprinkle laughter in every glance.

Jumping jelly gives a bounce and sway,
As elastic rainbows fly away,
Through layers of quirkiness they glide,
In a tapestry of fun, oh what a ride!

The universe winks with a playful grin,
Inviting folks to come and spin,
In the dance of dimensions, all out of place,
Laughter echoes in the endless space!

Chasing Cosmic Dreams

In a realm where giggles leave a trail,
Space ships zoom on gummy whale,
With sprightly sprites and comic leaps,
Chasing dreams where laughter creeps.

Marshmallow comets whizz on by,
While candy canes form a taffy sky,
Cookies trade jokes with flirty stars,
As humor travels on Venus cars.

A dapper penguin in a tuxedo bright,
Waltzes with meteors in the night,
They trade their secrets, bold and clear,
While peanut butter whispers in your ear.

Join the chase, embrace the flight,
In this dreamy land, all spirits bright,
Where every giggle paints the scene,
And joy reclaims what might have been!

Revelry in the Radiant Realm

In a lively land of fluffy frowns,
Lemonade lakes and cupcake towns,
A walrus belts a pop song loud,
While turtles form a boisterous crowd.

Pancake clouds float overhead,
As dancing doughnuts spin instead,
With jellybeans that sprout like trees,
A funny sight that's sure to please.

A parade of socks on furry feet,
With comic hats that can't be beat,
They march through valleys of whipped cream,
In a realm where laughter reigns supreme.

So come along, don't be shy,
In this radiant realm, you can fly,
Where jokes bounce high and frowns can't dwell,
Join the revelry, all's swell!

Celestial Currents

In the sky, a rubber band,
Twists and flops, oh what a stand!
Stars are giggling, comets dance,
Gravity gone, let's take a chance.

Galaxies spin like carnival rides,
Space-time tickles, where fun collides!
Laughter echoes in cosmic streams,
Dreams are stitched with glittering seams.

Planets play tag in bright blue skies,
Jumpy moons with googly eyes!
Saturn's rings, a slide of fun,
Join the dance, everyone's spun!

Floating through with silly hats,
Whimsical paths like wobbly cats.
In this realm, chaos is king,
And laughter joins in everything!

Echoes from the Quantum Abyss

In the depths where quarks play games,
Bubbles pop with nonsense names.
Particles juggling with flair,
A ticklish universe, beyond compare!

A photon sneezes, light beams scatter,
A cosmic laugh, oh, what a clatter!
Atoms tumble, pirouette with glee,
In a quantum jig, come dance with me!

Electrons spin like tops on strings,
Whirling through all these funny things.
Every quirk, a joke well told,
In this abyss, the brave are bold!

With each wave, a chuckle springs,
The void is rich with whims and flings.
From the depths of all that's small,
Laughter echoes, embracing all!

Fanciful Fractal Journeys

Down the spiral, colors burst,
Patterns wiggle, oh, how they thirst!
A fractal feast, a wild parade,
Where every tiny piece is made.

Shapes doing pirouettes in rows,
Infinity's joke, as everyone knows.
Within each loop, a giggling sprite,
Every twist just feels so right!

Fanciful paths that loop and bend,
Fractals frolic, not a single end.
Join the ride on this jolly reel,
In the depths of fun, we start to feel!

From the chaos, laughter sings,
Mathematical jests have all the swings.
Join the dance, don't miss a beat,
In this world, the joy's complete!

Starlit Vortex Adventures

In a vortex of sparkle and light,
Stars are diving, what a sight!
Spinning in circles, dizzy and bold,
This zany trip never gets old!

Planets whirly with cotton candy,
Twirling around, so sweet and dandy!
Galactic giggles fill the air,
In this chaos, there's nothing to spare!

Jumping through space, a carnival spin,
Laughter erupts, let the fun begin!
With starlight as our bouncy ball,
In this vortex, we'll never fall!

So grab a comet, let's ride away,
In a cosmic whirl, we laugh and play.
With each class of stars that we see,
On this adventure, you're with me!

Temporal Tides

In a clock that tickles time,
Laughter flows like silly slime.
Past and future play tag at noon,
Chasing shadows 'neath a cartoon moon.

When seconds twist and bounce around,
Days become a merry-go-round.
Jumping jacks with cosmic flair,
We pirouette through cosmic air.

A wink from yesterday's grandchild,
Today's mishaps make us wild.
We giggle as we warp and bend,
Through hiccups, we will never end.

So grab your boots of spacetime thread,
Let's leap where silly dreams are shed.
Floating in a laugh-filled slide,
Who knew the universe could be this wide?

The Fabric of Fancies

We weave the stars with threads of fun,
Twinkling patterns, joy begun.
A patchwork quilt of giggle spree,
Stitches of dreams from A to Z.

With needles made of starlit dreams,
We craft our whims in cosmic beams.
Tangled laughter fills the air,
As fuzzballs bounce without a care.

A fabric soft with all our hopes,
It dances light, and wildly mopes.
Sewing each giggle, grin, and glee,
Creating worlds like you and me.

In the loom of space, we twine,
Threads that shimmer, twist, and shine.
We ride the waves of fancy's tide,
On this fabric, we will glide.

Galactic Giggles

Stars chuckle as they take a spin,
In a dance with chaos, they break in.
Comets racing, bursting bright,
Making wishes, nighty night!

Planets wear their silliest hats,
Joking around with cosmic cats.
Gravity's pull? Just a playful tease,
As we float on stardust with ease.

Lightyears whizz by in a blur,
With giggles echoing, we concur.
The cosmos laughs in a cosmic shake,
Juggling planets, what a break!

So hop aboard this starry ride,
With humor as our constant guide.
Let's spiral through the cosmic ring,
In a universe where jokes take wing.

Surreal String Theory

Fingers plucking at cosmic strings,
Melodies of laughter as twilight sings.
Notes of whimsy dance in air,
The universe chuckles without a care.

Twisting spaces, bending lines,
Creating giggles in wacky designs.
A symphony of space-time curls,
As we twirl through surreal whirls.

With every tick, a funny flip,
Gravity gives us a silly grip.
In this theory, life's a jest,
Where every moment is a playful quest.

So let's embrace the vibrant play,
In this realm where jesters sway.
Together, we'll loop and spin,
In a world where humor's always in.

Charades of the Cosmos

In the void, stars play silly games,
Twinkling like lost socks in a breeze.
Galaxies dance with names like 'Fames,'
And planets juggle with quirky ease.

Asteroids laugh, they roll and glide,
Meteorites gossip in playful flight.
A comet slips, whoops, takes a ride,
On a noodle made of starlit light.

Aliens in capes throw glittery pies,
The moons moonwalk, giving a show.
With each bright burst, a silly surprise,
As they party where the starlight flows.

In this cosmic circus of fun and cheer,
Even black holes grin, with secrets to share.
So join the dance, dismiss all fear,
For once you start, you'll be floating there.

Serendipity in Starfields

Under skies where dreams collide,
Stars pop out like tricks from hats.
In constellations, odd shapes reside,
Like cats with wings and playful bats.

A planet winks with a cheeky glow,
While comets giggle on their twisty path.
Space is a stage with a cosmic show,
Create your own fun and feel the laugh!

Nebulas swirl in colors bright,
Dancing like friends at a festive game.
Shooting stars bloom in the velvet night,
Each wish a chuckle, never the same.

Laughter echoes through the vast unknown,
Gravity teases, it pulls you near.
In starfields, joy is freely sown,
So grab each giggle, hold it dear!

The Celestial Playwright

In the theater of sky, the scripts are unique,
A star plays a villain, oh what a scene!
The sun takes a bow, quite proud in its peak,
While planets rehearse, all feeling serene.

A black hole's a comedian, swallows the light,
While moons toss pies in an orbit of fun.
Galactic stories twist left and right,
As laughter erupts with each cosmic pun.

The stage is a canvas where chaos ignites,
With characters jumping through time and space.
Each act brings a giggle as laughter invites,
In this cosmic play, there's no need for grace!

Celestial scripts are absurd, yet bold,
With jokes that echo in ripples of glee.
So sit back and watch as the universe told,
Unfolds with the whimsy of endless spree.

Kaleidoscopic Jump

Jump through colors in a dreamy swirl,
Each flicker a giggle, each twist a grin.
Far-off worlds in a playful whirl,
As rainbows bounce where day begins.

Nebulae burst in a polka dot dance,
While stardust tickles the backs of dreams.
Every leap feels like a joyful chance,
Creating a laughter that brightly beams.

Comets zip by in their best attire,
With streamers trailing in zany trails.
Space is a ride on a cosmic tire,
Where whimsy and wonder never fail.

Join the parade of the chromatic delight,
Where galaxies giggle and twirl around.
In this kaleidoscope, we find our light,
A wonderfully silly universe found!

Cosmic Calypso

In the vastness of space, a dance takes flight,
Stars in tutus spin, in the soft moonlight.
Planets wear hats, what a curious sight,
Gravity giggles, as it pulls them tight.

Asteroids play maracas, comets jive,
Martians do the cha-cha, oh how they thrive!
Jupiter's on bongos, it's quite the hive,
In this cosmic party, all creatures arrive.

Neptune sips a cocktail, garnished with ice,
While Saturn's rings twirl, oh so precise.
Galaxies are spinning, never think twice,
Comets crack jokes, that's their own device.

Everyone's laughing in this starry sea,
As laughter echoes through infinity.
We dance among stars, wild and free,
In this cosmic calypso, just you and me.

The Orchestra of Oddity

In the galaxy's hall, where no one can hear,
An orchestra plays, spreading joy and cheer.
Celestial strings strummed by stars up high,
While planets hum softly, oh me, oh my!

A trumpet made of stardust blares out loud,
While black holes clap, oh, isn't it proud?
Nebulas swirl in colors unbowed,
With music that attracts quite the strange crowd.

Quasars twinkle like shiny disco balls,
Eclipses dance, answering cosmic calls.
Saturn swings bass, while Pluto recalls,
The sound of a giggle as gravity falls.

Jokes fly like confetti in nebular skies,
As comets play flutes with a glittering rise.
In this quirky concert where laughter complies,
The orchestra's charm is a sweet surprise.

Threads of Time and Laughter

Time spins like cotton candy, oh what a treat,
As laughs thread together, in rhythms so sweet.
Moments are sparkles, like stars that we meet,
Stitching together, life's bizarre beat.

Past tickles future with playful delight,
As echoes of laughter spin into the night.
Giggles weave patterns, shimmers of bright,
In a tapestry woven, where all feels right.

Chrono-pranksters leap, giving time a nudge,
With silly surprises, they won't let us budge.
History chuckles, gives fate a small grudge,
In this dance of the ages, we never begrudge.

Mirth flows like rivers through fabric of yore,
Every tick of the clock brings us back for more.
Threads of laughter unite, and we soar,
In this whimsical journey, forever we explore.

The Comedy of Celestial Bodies

In a stage of the cosmos, where comets take flight,
Planets act silly under the night.
Stars audition for roles, much to our delight,
In the comedy club of the cosmic light.

The sun cracks a joke, and the moon rolls its eyes,
While Saturn's great rings spin tales unwise.
Asteroids laugh loudly, to no one's surprise,
In this stellar pulpit, humor just flies.

Uranus tells puns that really do stank,
As galaxies chuckle, bursting with prank.
While black holes keep secrets in their deep rank,
Leaving stardust behind, like a cosmic blank.

The universe giggles, a raucous affair,
With laughter and joy filling up the air.
In this cosmic cabaret, beyond compare,
The comedy of celestial bodies, we all share.

Whimsical Dimensions

In a world where socks can dance,
And teacups twirl in playful prance,
The skies rain jellybeans and cream,
Everyone laughs, it's quite the dream.

A cat in boots rides on a snail,
While fishy folks tell knock-knock tales,
The trees wear hats of candy fluff,
In this strange land, there's never enough.

The clocks run backward, time's a game,
Each tick is filled with giggles and fame,
We skip through rainbows, slide on pies,
With grinning squirrels who wear bow ties.

So join the fun in quirky space,
Where giggles float with elegant grace,
In every corner, joy abounds,
In this odd realm, silliness surrounds.

Twilight Tangles

In twilight's glow, the stars all grin,
As the moon does jiggle in a spin,
The frogs in crowns hold court at night,
Deciding who shall dance in flight.

A rambunctious breeze throws hats around,
With giggles sweet as candy sound,
While dandelions blow cheeky sighs,
Petals spin like tiny pies.

The owls wear glasses, reading books,
And giggly gnomes swap silly looks,
With every flutter, laughter flies,
In tangled tales beneath the skies.

So take a leap in funny dreams,
Where nothing's ever as it seems,
In twilight's arms, let laughter sway,
And dance until the break of day.

Celestial Nonsense

Stars wearing sneakers dance on beams,
While jellyfish play hopscotch with dreams,
Galaxies giggle in cosmic jest,
Their sparkly bodies, truly the best.

Comets in tutus twirl with flair,
As aliens share the funniest hair,
Black holes giggle, 'Come take a ride!',
Through cosmic giggles, we slide and glide.

Asteroids playing tag, what fun!
With every drift, the laughter's spun,
A parade of planets, bright and round,
In this sky, pure joy is found.

So float on clouds of sweet delight,
In this whimsical, starry night,
Where every wisp brings a grin or two,
In the universe's humorous view.

Jesters of the Universe

The jesters twirl in zero-grav,
With jokes and pranks to make you laugh,
Each bow and cap a sight to see,
In colorful hues, oh what glee!

Planets juggle with dexterous flair,
As comets paint the sky with care,
With witty banter all around,
It's a circus show that knows no bound.

The suns throw pies at passing moons,
And laughter hums familiar tunes,
Each star a glittering, joking friend,
In this cosmic circus that won't end.

So join the jesters in their spree,
And chuckle with the galaxy,
In this merry flick of cosmic play,
The universe laughs in a joyful way.

The Curiosities of Cosmic Curves

In a twisty turn of space and time,
Dancing aliens play in their prime.
They wear odd socks and mismatched shoes,
Chasing shooting stars, they cannot lose.

A comet sneezes, bursts of light,
The universe giggles at this sight.
Planets wobble, they do a jig,
While asteroids boogie, oh so big.

Galactic cats with tails like streams,
Chasing after interstellar dreams.
They knock over moons, what a messy game,
Yet every flop, they find it's the same.

Through the cosmic soup, they swirl and spin,
With laughter echoing where they've been.
Each blink of an eye, a new surprise,
In the curious bends of the starry skies.

Spirals of Surreal Sorcery

In the land where gravity takes a break,
Bouncing bunnies dance, make no mistake.
They hop in circles, twisting quite wide,
Their laughter echoes, a merry ride.

With wands of licorice, they cast a spell,
Mighty rainbows emerge, oh so swell.
Unicorns giggle as they join the fun,
Painting the cosmos under the sun.

Time takes a nap, it rolls on a chair,
While stars unfold like socks in the air.
Each twirl reveals a silly charade,
In the magical mess that they've made.

As the ground starts to wiggle and quake,
All the chocolate rivers begin to shake.
Yet in their hearts, it's pure delight,
In spirals of whimsy, they take flight.

Beyond the Boundless Skies

Beyond the skies, where ducks can fly,
With googly eyes and a curious sigh.
They quack their tunes to a starry beat,
And slide on rainbows with twinkling feet.

Clouds turn into fluffy cotton balls,
Hosting tea parties in cosmic halls.
Aliens munching on jelly beans,
Creating chaos in their moonlit scenes.

Galaxies giggle, stretching their arms,
While space-time tickles with its funny charms.
Every moment's a dance, don't be forlorn,
In the laughter-filled space where dreams are born.

And when a meteor makes a wish,
They toss it back into the cosmic dish.
Oh, the sights they see, the tales to tell,
In realms where whimsy and wonders dwell.

Whirlwinds of Wonder

In whirlwinds of joy, the stars collide,
Jellyfish angels take a wild ride.
They sway through the cosmos, twinkling bright,
As giggles cascade on a moonbeam's light.

Whirling and twirling, the galaxies spin,
While mice in spacesuits dance with a grin.
Cosmic pies fly past in a sugary swoosh,
Tickling comets with a fluffy push.

Colors explode like fireworks at play,
Painting the universe all night and day.
Dancing quarks in a fizzy delight,
In a cosmic carnival, what a sight!

So grab your hats, and join the spree,
In a universe where everything's free.
With laughter and play, let's take flight,
In the whirlwinds of wonder, all feels just right.

Vortex of Vividness

In a twirl of colors bright,
Rabbits hop through day and night,
They wear hats that spin and twirl,
As they leap and twist and whirl.

Fish fly by on feathered wings,
Juggling clocks and other things,
A dance of laughter fills the air,
With giggles flowing everywhere.

The sun melts into a candy sky,
While frogs in tuxes start to fly,
They sing songs about the moon,
In a chorus that makes hearts swoon.

A maze made out of gumdrop trees,
Whispers secrets in the breeze,
Each turn a surprise awaits,
Where smiling koalas navigate.

Enigmatic Eclipses

A shadow plays upon the ground,
With whispers that make no sound,
Cats in bow ties twist and twine,
Looking for lost socks, oh so fine!

A hamster spins through cosmic dust,
In a rocket built for wild gusts,
They giggle as they zoom and glide,
With cupcake trails left far and wide.

The moon takes selfies with the stars,
As comets dance like poplar guitars,
Each snap a chuckle, joy unbound,
In this peculiar playground found.

A kaleidoscope of giggles fair,
Beaming brightly out of nowhere,
Unruly fun within the night,
In tides of dreams, we take flight.

Quantum Fairytales

A kingdom locked in quantum states,
Where jellybeans guard candy gates,
Knights on skates with shields so bright,
Shade their eyes from frosted light.

The queen is made of fluffy cream,
A ruler of the sweetest dream,
Her crown adorned with gummy bears,
While giggling elves dance down the stairs.

Dragons breathe out fizzy cheers,
As they toast with fizzy beers,
Each tale spins a comic twist,
In laughter's brave, enchanted mist.

With every page a whirl of fun,
The sparkles dance just like the sun,
Each story holds a spark of grace,
A giggle echoed in this place.

Whirlwinds of Wonder

In a vortex of bright balloon,
A playful cat plays a tune,
Socks become the stars tonight,
As they twirl in sheer delight.

A dash of spice and a flick of flair,
Who knew time could twist like hair?
Bouncing on rainbows, oh so free,
Where giggles swirl like honeybee.

Silly hats on dancing trees,
Turning whispers into breezy tease,
A whirlwind of laughter fills the sky,
Let's skip and jump, oh my, oh my!

With every gust of playful wind,
A tale of cheer begins to spin,
In this carnival of fate and fun,
We chase the moon till the day is done.

Echoes of Astral Amusements

In a realm where jokes take flight,
Atoms dance and fizz with light.
Galaxies twirl in playful glee,
Stars strum laughter's melody.

Chasing comets, we skip and run,
Splitting atoms, oh what fun!
A cosmic jest in every twist,
Laughter trails, we can't resist.

Floating dreams and silly sights,
Cosmic jests that spark delight.
Planets giggle, moons engage,
In this universe, we turn the page.

Catch a nebula's winking eye,
As comical quarks float on by.
With each flash of starlit glow,
Jokes are spun, the laughter flows.

Stars That Giggle

Twinkling lights with winks of fun,
A galaxy of puns has begun.
Meteor showers rain down glee,
As we dance in zero gravity.

Planets chuckle in their orbits,
Gravity's pull can't tame their wit.
Supernova sparks a bright laugh,
While comets make a comical graph.

Saturn's rings twist in delight,
As asteroids frolic in the night.
Alien creatures play hide and seek,
With a wink, a smirk, a giggle, a tweak.

The universe unfolds its game,
In each star, we find a name.
A celestial circus spins and twirls,
As laughter sails through starry pearls.

Cosmic Capers

In the vastness where giggles soar,
Planets at play, forevermore.
Time loops dance like a silly prank,
In this cosmic, jolly rank.

Stars ride comets, a joyful race,
With winked eyes and a silly face.
Galactic gags, a laugh parade,
In the void, our joy is made.

Quasars quip in a dazzling hue,
While black holes play peek-a-boo.
Each pulsar ticks to a playful beat,
As stardust giggles light our street.

Gravity tricks and swirling spins,
In this realm where humor wins.
So grab a laugh, take a leap,
In the cosmic capers, joy runs deep.

Enchanted Echoes

In a space where echoes play,
Wit resounds in a bright array.
Shooting stars bring giddy glee,
As the cosmos hums a melody.

Ethereal whispers tease our minds,
With hilarious truths from starlit binds.
A galaxy giggles, swirls around,
In each twinkling joke, joy is found.

Nebulas glow with cheerful flair,
As silly banter fills the air.
Constellations share their jests,
In this realm, humor never rests.

So float along in dreams so bright,
Where laughter sparkles in the night.
In the echoes of the cosmic sphere,
A universe of fun draws near.

The Enigmas of Existence

In a universe full of quirks,
Where ducks wear hats and dance like jerks,
A cat on a moonbeam starts to prance,
While jellybeans hold the cosmic chance.

Time tickles clocks with sandy toes,
As giggles sprout from the black hole's throes,
A pizza slice spins through the void,
In this riddle, we're all overjoyed.

Stars wink as they sip fizzy drinks,
Planets laugh at our earnest blinks,
A koala on Mars plays poker games,
And we ponder the universe's strange names.

So come join this quirky parade,
Where every logic's beautifully swayed,
In a dance of oddities, we glide,
In this jester's realm, let joy reside.

Portals of Possibility

A door swings open with a squeaky plea,
To lands where fish wear hats made of brie,
Jump through a window, land on a cloud,
Where unicorns giggle and rainbows are loud.

A toaster sings as it pops out toast,
While space cows dance, they'll surely boast,
The sky bends and stretches, oh what a sight,
As jellyfish float in the glow of twilight.

Underneath trees where candy grows,
They hold secrets that nobody knows,
Chasing fireflies with a net in hand,
In this whimsical universe, we take a stand.

So leap through the portals, embrace the bizarre,
In lands where laughter is the brightest star,
For every twist, there's a chuckle to find,
In the realms of the silly, we're all intertwined.

Mirth among the Milky Ways

Zany critters hop between the stars,
With marshmallow fields and chocolate bars,
Giggles echo through the cosmic night,
As comets twirl in a feather-light flight.

A quiz with aliens, who wear flip-flops,
They quiz us on life as we eat lollipops,
Why do giraffes wear polka dots, they ask,
In nonsense we find our delightful task.

Glimpses of laughter filter through space,
Where dreams skip and twirl in a playful race,
Bubblegum planets spin sweet melodies,
As happiness buzzes like busy bees.

In the dance of the stars, we spin with glee,
As mischief makes merry for you and me,
Each laugh illuminated by beams from afar,
In the mirth of the Milky Ways, we're the star.

Conundrums of Cosmic Color

A canvas sprawls in the twilight gleam,
Where purple elephants play in a dream,
With crayons made of dewdrops and cheer,
Conundrums ripple, giggles draw near.

Improbable hues swirl in the sky,
As polka-dotted rain falls down from high,
Green giraffes roll in the grass with delight,
While philosophical squirrels ponder the night.

Whirligig galaxies dance hand in hand,
As laughter erupts across this grand land,
Mysteries wrapped in a joke and a pun,
In this kaleidoscope, life's never done.

So throw all your worries into the stars,
Embrace the oddity that colors our scars,
In the vibrant tapestry, we all must find,
The funny enigmas that weave through the mind.

Ethereal Antics

In a place where giggles float,
Fish wear hats, and cows can gloat.
Socks dance wildly, walls are spry,
Chasing dreams in a candy sky.

Balloons have secrets they won't share,
They giggle softly in the air.
Jumping beans play leapfrog on,
A pickle dressed as a leprechaun.

Clouds are ticklish, twirling about,
While the sun sneezes, silly shout!
Mice in glasses solving a puzzle,
Creating giggles, watch the muzzle.

At dusk, frogs don their finest ties,
To host a dance beneath the fries.
In this wacky world, laughter rings,
Where nonsense reigns, and joy takes wings.

The Kaleidoscope of Imagined Cosmos

Stars wear pajamas in shades of mint,
While comets skedaddle in a pink glint.
Galaxy cupcakes float on by,
With sprinkles of laughter in the sky.

Planets juggle in cosmic glee,
One spilled stardust - oh, what a spree!
Space whales sing a silly tune,
Bouncing frantically to the moon.

Nebulae swirl in polka dot hats,
And dancing robots are charming cats.
Through spacetime giggles play peek-a-boo,
In a place where everything's askew.

Infinity's a whimsical game,
The universe's pulse is never the same.
So hop on a comet, let laughter guide,
In this kaleidoscope, come take a ride!

Fluctuations of Fantasy

Ants in tutus prance on the floor,
While a lion plays piano, what a roar!
A rabbit with glasses reads a book,
As a duck in a coat gives you a look.

Frogs in top hats leap through the air,
Playing hopscotch without a care.
A snail on a skateboard goes for a spin,
While a turtle declares, 'I'm winning!'

Lollipops whisper secrets so sly,
As marshmallows float and pie in the sky.
Jellybeans giggling, parade down the lane,
In a carnival world, joy is the gain!

With each wrapper popped, surprise unfolds,
In this land where laughter beholds.
The fluctuations dance in whimsical grace,
Through the quirky, animated space.

Celestial Stockroom

In a stockroom filled with dreams and charms,
Socks are bouncing, with joyful arms.
Rubber ducks sail on barrels of cheese,
Giggling stars float with playful ease.

A cupboard of jokes spills out in heaps,
As silly whispers weave through the peeps.
A ladder of clouds leans against the wall,
While cupcakes trade secrets, one and all.

Boxes of giggles stacked to the sky,
With every tickle, the planets sigh.
Cacti in hats join in the cheer,
In this stockroom of whimsy, let's have a beer!

Navigating through laughter's delight,
Cosmic shenanigans burst into light.
So choose your treasure – humor or fun,
In the celestial stockroom, all can run!

Temporal Trials

In a time loop, I ate a shoe,
Each bite made me feel so blue.
I tried to dance, but tripped again,
Who knew time had such a funny bend?

I met a cat who wore a hat,
He spoke to me; imagine that!
He said, 'Don't rush, just take your time,'
But I was stuck in this silly rhyme.

The clock struck thirteen, what a sight,
I laughed so hard, it felt just right.
With every tick, I'd jump and sway,
In this odd dance, I'll stay all day.

I flew through past with a polka dot,
And landed here—it's quite the plot!
With each new turn, I grin and swirl,
In time's amusement park, life's a whirl.

Fractured Realities

In a world where ducks wear shoes,
They quack in rhythm, sharing news.
I tried to understand their dance,
But all I did was take a chance.

The sky turned purple, grass was blue,
I asked a frog, 'Is this all true?'
He winked and said, 'It's all a game,
Just play along, and miss the blame.'

A fish in tux, he sang a song,
Of spaceships and where they belong.
With every note, my worries flee,
As I chase dreams in this wild spree.

Reality bends like a gummy worm,
Twisting and turning without concern.
Laughing gas fills this fractured space,
In every twist, I find my place.

Whims of the Infinite

Beyond the stars, there's ice cream rain,
Sweet, sticky cosmos, a dessert terrain.
I scooped the sky with a waffle cone,
In this vast space, I'm never alone.

Galaxies giggle as they spin 'round,
With every turn, new friends abound.
The sun wears shades, he's quite a sight,
Chasing comets, oh, what a flight!

Tickling planets with jellybean dust,
In this comedy, I place my trust.
Each twist and turn, a new delight,
In the whims of space, I take my flight.

From asteroids shaped like rubber ducks,
To moons that chat and share their luck.
With laughter echoing through the void,
These cosmic shenanigans can't be destroyed.

The Laughter of Lightyears

In a spaceship made of candy bars,
I'm zipping past the twinkling stars.
With every bite, my joy expands,
In this sweet journey, I make demands.

Lightyears giggle as I zoom along,
Each moment feels like a merry song.
The universe winks, a cheeky play,
With time and space at bay today.

Riding beams of bright, I twirl and glide,
Under the comets, I swiftly slide.
Each chuckle echoes through the void,
In laughter's grip, I am overjoyed.

Stardust sprinkles on my head,
In this cosmic playground, I'm well-fed.
With every laugh, the cosmos cheers,
For in this voyage, we shed our fears.

Luminous Labyrinths

In a maze made of twinkling lights,
Bouncing about in curious flights,
Each corner hides a giggle or two,
Chasing shadows that dance and woo.

Muffled whispers float in the air,
Nonsense words without a care,
A cat with goggles sips on tea,
While a mouse wears boots, wild and free.

There's a rocket made of candy bars,
Zooming past bananas and toy cars,
Frogs in tuxedos leap and laugh,
Pirates toast with fizzy giraffe.

Twirl and spin through this jolly game,
Where nothing's ever quite the same,
With a wink and a nod from a starry friend,
The silliness knows no end.

The Glee of Gravity's Games

Floating high, a trampoline kite,
Bouncing up with sheer delight,
The ground below holds giggling dreams,
In this realm, nothing's as it seems.

Pies rain down like bursts of cheer,
Catch them home before they veer,
A jellyfish does the hula hoop,
While raccoons join in, forming a troupe.

In this dance of gravity's sway,
Bubbles burst, igniting play,
A tree sprinkles popcorn from above,
Casting giggles, a show of love.

Laughter echoes around the bend,
As silly races never end,
Float on smiles, the world aglow,
In this fun place, let's steal the show!

Chronicles of Celestial Charisma

Stars wear hats, oh so bright,
Winking down with pure delight,
Jupiter juggles meteors fast,
While Saturn spins, a ringed contrast.

On a comet's tail, the dance begins,
Wormy worms don brightly colored skins,
Pastel unicorns prance with glee,
In this story, all are free.

Asteroids roll with silly grace,
Chasing a sunbeam, a silly race,
Galactic kittens chase a beam,
In the cosmos, they live the dream.

Join the fun, the celestial play,
Where the moonlight sings and sways,
With every twirl, a fresh surprise,
Mysteries lie behind those friendly skies.

The Drama of Divergent Paths

On a path where bananas grow,
Flip-flop shoes dance to and fro,
A turtle races, slow but sure,
While rabbits giggle, they can't endure.

Two signs queuing for a fun ride,
One says 'chocolate,' the other 'slide,'
Choose your fate, either taste or play,
With every step, the weird ballet.

A broomstick flies, a cat gets lost,
Turning back, it meets a frost,
A bubblegum tree sways its branches,
Dancing squirrels take their chances.

In this story, twist and twirl,
Every choice spins and unfurls,
A whimsical place where laughter reigns,
Adventures burst like sunny trains.

Dreamweaver's Portal

In a swirl of colors bright,
I found a door to endless night.
A sock flew past, it waved hello,
As giggles echoed, high and low.

With jellybeans and bouncing stars,
We danced on clouds, oh what bizarre!
A rabbit rode a unicycle,
Telling jokes with every cycle.

The clocks ticked backward, time took flight,
As I chased a cat that glowed with light.
He spoke in rhymes, it was such a treat,
Wearing a hat, oh so sweet!

In the realm of dreams, we twirled and spun,
Every mishap delivered fun.
With laughter bursting at the seams,
I drifted off, lost in dreams.

The Astral Amusement Park

Step right up to the cosmic fair,
Where candy comets float in air.
An octopus plays the banjo loud,
While ducks make up a giggling crowd.

The roller coaster's made of light,
We zipped through space, oh what a flight!
A cotton candy nebula spun,
Left my mouth agape, oh what fun!

Swinging on a swing of meteors,
Spinning tales of galactic wars.
A giant squirrel served lemonade,
As laughter bubbled, worries we slayed.

The carousel spun with planets bright,
Each creature danced in pure delight.
With every laugh, we soared and glowed,
In the park where joy overflows.

Spirals of Serendipity

In a twist of fate, I bumped a cloud,
Which giggled softly, oh so loud.
It spun me 'round in a silly reel,
As popcorn stars began to peel.

A snail in shades slid by with flair,
Claiming he'd raced the moonlit air.
With laughter bubbling like a stream,
We shared stories woven with dreams.

The daisies danced in toe-to-toe,
With melodies only they could know.
While squirrels in pajamas joined the fun,
Their cartwheels made every heart run.

In spirals twisting, bright and free,
I found my joy in the cosmic spree.
With each wild turn, a new delight,
In the madcap swirl of endless night.

Laughter in the Void

In the space between the beats of time,
I tripped on stardust, fell in rhyme.
A fish on bicycles whizzed past me,
Casting jokes as they sailed through sea.

The darkness giggled, what a surprise!
With winks and grins, it filled the skies.
A witty ghost played tricks galore,
Telling puns that made spirits roar.

In the void, we tossed our cares,
And danced with beams from other squares.
With bubbles of laughter, we took flight,
Chasing shadows in pure delight.

As echoes rang from star to star,
I knew this chaos was bizarre.
In the void where laughter resides,
A grin spreads wide as joy abides.

Infinity's Playground

In a space made of giggles, where laughter can soar,
Bouncing on starlight, who could ask for more?
Comets tumble and dance, juggling meteors bright,
A cosmic carnival, oh what a sight!

Planets play hopscotch across the vast sky,
With aliens as judges, they're giving a try.
Stars spin like tops, while moons do the twist,
In this boundless playground, no fun can be missed!

Gravity's forgotten, we're free to just glide,
Joyrides on rainbows, with space squirrels inside.
Black holes in this region are just rides in disguise,
Where upside-down smiles greet you with surprise!

So hold onto your hats, as we whirl and we zoom,
In this infinite space filled with laughter and bloom.
Every tickle of stardust will leave you aglow,
A universe chuckling, come join in the show!

Parallel Dreams

In a realm where the silly meets serious thought,
The birds wear top hats, oh what have we caught?
Kittens in spacesuits explore the unknown,
While turtles in bow ties spin tales of their own.

Across realms of giggles, where shadows can smile,
A curious gnome rides a cat for a mile.
Pancakes are planets, syrup rivers flow,
In this strange moonlit world, whimsical wonders grow.

Dancing on clouds made of cotton and cream,
The absurdity reigns in this flickering dream.
Wizards do jiggles while fairies make pies,
In a paradox place where the outlandish flies!

So leap through dimensions, take flight with a grin,
In parallel dreams, let the fun truly begin.
For every twinkling star, there's a laugh left to share,
In the giggly cosmos, every moment is rare!

Wondrous Wormways

Through tunnels of tinsel and sparkly light,
Little creatures giggle, what a silly sight!
They travel with whimsy on trains made of cheese,
In this twisty dimension, you float with such ease.

Bouncing on rainbows, they slide and they glide,
Chasing after bubbles that bounce by their side.
A penguin on skates shimmies past with a cheer,
While juggling bright planets, oh my, what a sphere!

In the bend of a giggle, a riddle takes flight,
It flutters and flops in this marvelous night.
With each turn they take in this goofy parade,
Laughter erupts and worries just fade.

So join in the travels through pathways of cheer,
Where the funny unnerves all the serious fear.
A voyage through wonders, let silliness reign,
In the whims of the wormways, joy is our gain!

Celestial Comedy

In the theater of space, the stars take the stage,
With meteors acting, they're learning their age.
Comets write jokes in a swirling delight,
While the moons crack up under the soft starlight.

Galactic jesters flip through infinite shows,
Tickling quarks and the fabric that flows.
Laughter erupts from the heart of the void,
Where everything's crazy, and no one's annoyed!

The sun tells a story, its rays full of zest,
While black holes are laughing at all of the rest.
With space-time tickling their celestial feet,
Cosmic slapstick brings humor so sweet!

So gather your giggles, let's dance in the dark,
In this comical cosmos, be sure to embark.
For comedy reigns in the heavens above,
Where nonsense is king, and laughter's the love!

www.ingramcontent.com/pod-product-compliance
Lightning Source LLC
Chambersburg PA
CBHW071854160426
43209CB00003B/549